Your Government:
How It Works

# The History of the
# Democratic Party

Bruce & Becky Durost Fish

Arthur M. Schlesinger, jr.
**Senior Consulting Editor**

Chelsea House Publishers
Philadelphia

CHELSEA HOUSE PUBLISHERS
*Editor in Chief* Stephen Reginald
*Production Manager* Pamela Loos
*Art Director* Sara Davis
*Director of Photography* Judy L. Hasday
*Managing Editor* James D. Gallagher
*Senior Production Editor* LeeAnne Gelletly

Staff for THE HISTORY OF THE DEMOCRATIC PARTY
*Project Editor/Publishing Coordinator* Jim McAvoy
*Associate Art Director* Takeshi Takahashi
*Series Designer* Takeshi Takahashi, Keith Trego

The Chelsea House World Wide Web address is
http://www.chelseahouse.com

3 5 7 9 8 6 4 2

Library of Congress Cataloging-in-Publication Data

Fish, Bruce.
    The history of the Democratic Party / by Bruce and
    Becky Durost Fish.
        p. cm. — (Your government—how it works)
    Includes bibliographical references.
    Summary: Traces the origins of the Democratic Party, dis-
cussing key figures, conventions, platforms, and its organization.
    ISBN 0-7910-5539-6 (hc)
    1. Democratic Party (U.S.)—Juvenile literature—History.
[1. Democratic Party (U.S.) 2. Political parties.] I. Fish, Becky
Durost II. Title. III. Series.

JK2316 .F55 1999
324.2736'09—dc21                                    99-049070

# Contents

YOUR GOVERNMENT
HOW IT WORKS

# Introduction

# Government: Crises of Confidence

## Arthur M. Schlesinger, jr.

FROM THE START, Americans have regarded their government with a mixture of reliance and mistrust. The men who founded the republic understood the importance of government. "If men were angels," observed the 51st Federalist Paper, "no government would be necessary." But men are not angels. Because human beings are subject to wicked as well as to noble impulses, government was deemed essential to assure freedom and order.

The American revolutionaries, however, also knew that government could become a source of injury and oppression. The men who gathered in Philadelphia in 1787 to write the Constitution therefore had two purposes in mind: They wanted to establish a strong central authority and to limit that central authority's capacity to abuse its power.

To prevent the abuse of power, the Founding Fathers wrote two basic principles into the Constitution. The principle of federalism divided power between the state governments and the central authority. The principle of the separation of powers subdivided the central authority itself into three branches—the executive, the legislative, and the judiciary—so that "each may be a check on the other."

YOUR GOVERNMENT: HOW IT WORKS examines some of the major parts of that central authority, the federal government. It explains how various officials, agencies, and departments operate and explores the political organizations that have grown up to serve the needs of government.

## Introduction

The federal government as presented in the Constitution was more an idealistic construct than a practical administrative structure. It was barely functional when it came into being.

This was especially true of the executive branch. The Constitution did not describe the executive branch in any detail. After vesting executive power in the president, it assumed the existence of "executive departments" without specifying what these departments should be. Congress began defining their functions in 1789 by creating the Departments of State, Treasury, and War.

President Washington, assisted by Secretary of the Treasury Alexander Hamilton, equipped the infant republic with a working administrative structure. Congress also continued that process by creating more executive departments as they were needed.

Throughout the 19th century, the number of federal government workers increased at a consistently faster rate than did the population. Increasing concerns about the politicization of public service led to efforts—bitterly opposed by politicians—to reform it in the latter part of the century.

The 20th century saw considerable expansion of the federal establishment. More importantly, it saw growing impatience with bureaucracy in society as a whole.

The Great Depression during the 1930s confronted the nation with its greatest crisis since the Civil War. Under Franklin Roosevelt, the New Deal reshaped the federal government, assigning it a variety of new responsibilities and greatly expanding its regulatory functions. By 1940, the number of federal workers passed the 1 million mark.

Critics complained of big government and bureaucracy. Business owners resented federal regulation. Conservatives worried about the impact of paternalistic government on self-reliance, on community responsibility, and on economic and personal freedom.

When the United States entered World War II in 1941, government agencies focused their energies on supporting the war effort. By the end of World War II, federal civilian employment had risen to 3.8 million. With peace, the federal establishment declined to around 2 million in 1950. Then growth resumed, reaching 2.8 million by the 1980s.

A large part of this growth was the result of the national government assuming new functions such as: affirmative action in civil rights, environmental protection, and safety and health in the workplace.

Some critics became convinced that the national government was a steadily growing behemoth swallowing up the liberties of the people. The 1980s brought new intensity to the debate about government growth. Foes of Washington bureaucrats preferred local government, feeling it more responsive to popular needs.

But local government is characteristically the government of the locally powerful. Historically, the locally powerless have often won their human and constitutional rights by appealing to the national government. The national government has defended racial justice against local bigotry, upheld the Bill of Rights against local vigilantism, and protected natural resources from local greed. It has civilized industry and secured the rights of labor organizations. Had the states' rights creed prevailed, perhaps slavery would still exist in the United States.

Americans are still of two minds. When pollsters ask large, spacious questions—Do you think government has become too involved in your lives? Do you think government should stop regulating business?—a sizable majority opposes big government. But when asked specific questions about the practical work of government—Do you favor Social Security? Unemployment compensation? Medicare? Health and safety standards in factories? Environmental protection?—a sizable majority approves of intervention.

We do not like bureaucracy, but we cannot live without it. We need its genius for organizing the intricate details of our daily lives. Without bureaucracy, modern society would collapse. It would be impossible to run any of the large public and private organizations we depend on without bureaucracy's division of labor and hierarchy of authority. The challenge is to keep these necessary structures of our civilization flexible, efficient, and capable of innovation.

More than 200 years after the drafting of the Constitution, Americans still rely on government but also mistrust it. These attitudes continue to serve us well. What we mistrust, we are more likely to monitor. And government needs our constant attention if it is to avoid inefficiency, incompetence, and arbitrariness. Without our informed participation, it cannot serve us individually or help us as a people to attain the lofty goals of the Founding Fathers.

*James Madison (bottom) and Thomas Jefferson (top), are considered to be the fathers of the Democratic Party. They wanted to balance Alexander Hamilton's desire to make the national government strong and state governments weak with their own "republican interest," where the rights of all individuals are represented by government.*

**CHAPTER** 1

# The Party That Wanted to Die

## The Early Years

THE LAST THING Thomas Jefferson and James Madison wanted to do was create a political party. In the 1790s people called political parties factions. They believed parties were made up of men who wanted to get rich at the expense of everyone else in a nation. The United States, at that time, had no political parties.

Thomas Jefferson and James Madison, however, had a problem. President George Washington got most of his advice from Alexander Hamilton, who served on the president's cabinet. Hamilton was doing everything he could to make the national government strong and the state governments weak. He tried to make things better for industry and commerce, but he wasn't interested in helping farmers. These policies helped northern states and hurt southern states. Even federal taxes collected in the South were being used to help the North.

Alexander Hamilton's policies worried Thomas Jefferson and James Madison. They thought that if the national government became too strong, individual people would lose their rights. They feared that Alexander Hamilton and his friends would bring tyranny to their new nation. They hadn't fought the Revolutionary War so that new leaders could treat people just as badly as Britain's King George III had treated the colonies. In addition, they didn't want the southern states to become so unhappy that they would break off from the United States and start a new nation.

Thomas Jefferson was also on the president's cabinet, but George Washington didn't listen to Jefferson as much as he listened to Hamilton. Jefferson and Madison decided that the only way to overturn Hamilton's policies was through Congress.

## The Republican Interest

James Madison was good at getting government leaders to work together. He persuaded a group of southern congressmen to vote with him against Hamilton's policies. They began to call themselves "the republican interest" because they were fighting to make sure the United States remained a **republic.** In a republic, everyone is represented in the government. "The republican interest" didn't want one person or even a small group of people controlling everything.

At that time the United States had only one national paper. It was run by friends of Hamilton. Jefferson and Madison decided that they needed to have a national paper that spoke for "the republican interest." They asked the poet Philip Freneau to start a newspaper that would report stories from their point of view.

The first issue of the *National Gazette* was published on October 31, 1791. It included attacks on Hamilton's policies. For the first time the republican point of view was being heard across the nation.

In spite of publicity from this newspaper and Madison's hard work, there weren't enough votes in Congress to overturn Hamilton's policies. Hamilton's opponents, however, had another idea. George Washington had decided not to seek a third term as president in 1796. Members of "the republican interest" decided to have Thomas Jefferson run for president. Aaron Burr from New York was also asked to run.

By this time the members of "the republican interest" were calling themselves the Republican Party. Although the name is the same, this Republican Party had no connection to today's Republican Party.

## The Federalists

Hamilton and his supporters, in turn, began calling themselves Federalists, because they wanted to strengthen the role of the federal government. They asked John Adams and Thomas Pinckney to run for president against Jefferson and Burr.

*Alexander Hamilton, first secretary of the treasury and one of President George Washington's chief advisors. Hamilton, the leader of the Federalists, wanted a strong national government tied to people of wealth and to industrial interests.*

At this early period in American history, presidents and vice presidents were chosen by the **electoral college,** made up of representatives from each state. These electors each cast votes for two **candidates,** but they didn't specify which person they preferred for president and which for vice president. Whoever got the most votes became president. The second highest vote-getter became vice president.

Because a two-party system didn't exist when the United States was first formed, the 1796 election had strange results. Federalist John Adams was elected president, and Republican Thomas Jefferson was elected vice president.

At first, things seemed to be going well. President Adams wanted to play down the differences between the Federalists and the Republicans. He assured the people that he wanted a republican form of government, not an aristocracy or monarchy, as some of his enemies had claimed. He expressed a desire to develop a solid friendship between France and the United States. This surprised and pleased the Republicans because Federalists were known for not wanting to have anything to do with France.

Soon, however, problems developed. The relationship with France soured. Then, in July 1798, Federalist leaders got Congress to pass the Sedition Act. This act prohibited any criticism of the American government or the president. People found guilty of breaking this law could be fined and thrown in jail.

The law was set to expire on March 3, 1801, the date when the next president would be inaugurated. In effect, the Sedition Act prevented Republicans from criticizing the policies of the Federalists. How could Republicans win elections if they couldn't point out areas where they thought the Federalists were in error?

## The Organization of the Republicans

The Republicans decided to work around the law. Directed by Thomas Jefferson, they organized their party into local committees that worked under state committees. The state committees got their orders from a national committee. This was the first time a national party in the United States was so well organized.

Republican newspapers defied the Sedition Act. They accused the government of placing heavy taxes on the people to support an expensive navy and army that were not fighting a war. They also objected to other government programs paid for by these taxes. Federalist attorneys tried to use the Sedition Act to silence the Republican newspapers, but it took so long to hold court cases that most newspapers were able to continue publishing their stories.

Once again, Jefferson and Adams ran for president. This time, Jefferson and his running mate Aaron Burr won the election. Party members still viewed the party as a necessary evil. They did not expect it to last.

Jefferson planned to destroy the party system by absorbing reasonable Federalists and their views into the larger whole. "Nothing shall be spared on my part," he wrote, "to obliterate the traces of party and consolidate the nation, if it can be done without the abandonment of principle."

In spite of his intentions, Jefferson was forced to be both president and party leader. Unlike today, cabinet officers didn't submit their resignations after a presidential election. Jefferson fired many of Adams's appointees and replaced them with Republicans.

The Republicans kept some Federalist policies, but they did not renew the Sedition Act. Jefferson freed the people who had been put in prison because of it. He also made sure that any fines they had paid were refunded.

During Jefferson's two terms of office, he oversaw the Louisiana Purchase. This territory more than doubled the size of the United States. He also pushed through funding for the Lewis and Clark expedition.

International affairs were more complicated. In 1803 Great Britain and France, under Napoleon Bonaparte, went

*The Lewis and Clark expedition was funded during Thomas Jefferson's terms of office. This recently discovered map may help historians find where the expedition spent the winter of 1805–1806.*

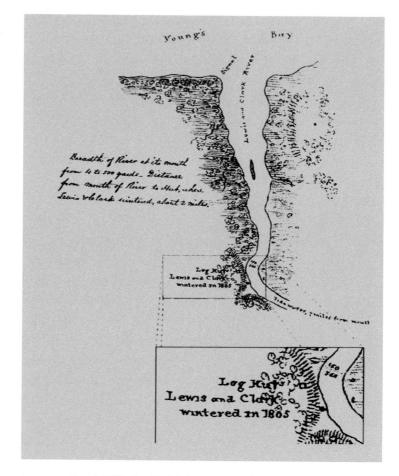

to war. By 1805 the British were seizing American ships that carried French goods. The French were seizing American ships that carried British goods. The British were also boarding American ships to capture British deserters. In the process they took many native-born Americans as well. This outraged the American public.

Rather than declare war, Jefferson closed American ports. This action only hurt American business and agriculture, because it cut off access to European trade. In March 1809 Jefferson signed an act that ended the embargo. It was one of his last acts as president. Republican James Madison became president that same month.

During the next three years, the Republican Party changed. By 1811, younger, pro-war Republicans began pressing for war against Great Britain. These congressmen were mostly from southern and western states. They wanted the United States to seize more land on the North American continent. They were very nationalistic and didn't care much about the states' rights issues that were so important to Thomas Jefferson and "the republican interest" back in the 1790s. These young Republicans saw war as an opportunity to claim more land for the United States.

Under pressure, Madison went to war in 1812. The war was unpopular in New England. Many aspects of it were a disaster. But after it was over, the pro-war Republicans were still popular. The economy was strong. Between 1816 and 1821, five new states entered the Union. The Republican Party still included farmers, but it now attracted manufacturers, factory workers, and other urban groups as well.

In 1817 Madison left office. Republican James Monroe became the new president. He is probably best known for the Monroe Doctrine. This doctrine stated that Europe and the Americas were two separate worlds. Europe should

*The* USS Constitution *defeats the British warship* Guerriere *in the War of 1812. Nicknamed "Old Ironsides," the* Constitution *was saved from destruction by public sentiment in 1833 and is maintained today at Boston navy yard in Massachusetts.*

not interfere in events in America, and America shouldn't be involved with events in Europe.

Nearing the end of his second term in 1824, Monroe hoped that William H. Crawford would be elected president. Four men in the Republican Party wanted to be president, however, and all four men ran. Andrew Jackson won the **popular vote,** but the electoral college failed to give any candidate a majority of its **electoral votes.** The election was decided in the House of Representatives, which declared John Quincy Adams, the son of John Adams, the new president. This turn of events completely divided the Republican Party.

*Andrew Jackson's 1815 victory over the British in the Battle of New Orleans. When Jackson was elected president in 1828, the Republican Party became known as the Democratic Party to represent Jackson's democratic beliefs.*

## Andrew Jackson and the Democratic Party

Over the next three years, Andrew Jackson united the party. In 1828 he was elected president. Unlike previous presidents, Andrew Jackson was not born into a wealthy family. He was born in poverty to Scotch-Irish immigrant parents and did not receive formal schooling. Largely self-

educated, he became a lawyer and soldier and then entered politics.

Because of his background, Jackson felt a responsibility to protect ordinary people from powerful business and government interests. His followers said that they stood for **democracy.** In a democracy everyone has a say in what the government does. The rich and powerful can't force their will on the poor and weak.

Because of its support of democracy, the Republican Party eventually became known as the Democratic Party. They wanted a smaller federal government so that individual states could have more power.

Acting as party leader, Andrew Jackson created the national party **convention.** He also introduced the idea of a **party platform.** When he left office in 1837, the Democratic Party was in good shape. Disagreements over slavery, however, were about to tear both the party and the nation apart.

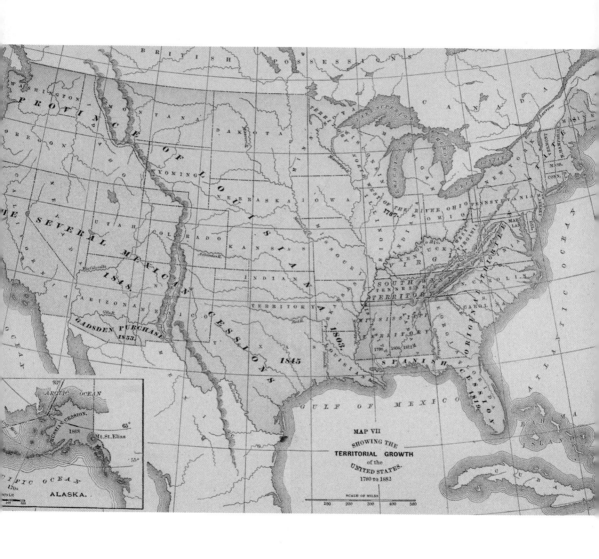

MAP VII
SHOWING THE
TERRITORIAL GROWTH
of the
UNITED STATES.
1780 to 1882

SCALE OF MILES
100    200    300    400    500

ALASKA.

*Slavery in the territories became a national issue in the 1840s, but it was less important to most Americans than expanding the nation. This map shows land gained by the United States in its war with Mexico (in pink at left).*

**CHAPTER 2**

# Fighting Over Slavery

### The Democrats Face the Whigs

IN MANY WAYS THE next 24 years were full of good news for the Democratic Party. Four Democratic presidents were elected. They were Martin Van Buren, James K. Polk, Franklin Pierce, and James Buchanan.

But the Democratic Party also faced difficulties. When Martin Van Buren became president in 1837, the country started having problems with money. People lost jobs; banks closed. Most people blamed the Democratic Party for the hard times because the president was a Democrat.

The members of the Democratic Party disagreed about how to fix the economy. The arguments became so violent that some Democrats left the party and joined the Whigs, the only other political party.

In 1840 it was time to elect a new president. The Democratic Party again chose Martin Van Buren as its candidate. The Whigs chose

*Whig William Henry
Harrison (pictured)
defeated Democrat
Martin Van Buren in
1840 by blaming the
nation's financial
problems on the
Democratic Party.*

William Henry Harrison, a military hero. For the first time, two political parties **campaigned** against each other all over the country.

The Whigs worked hard to convince people that their financial problems were caused by Democrats. They called President Van Buren "Martin Van Ruin." They chanted the slogan "Van, Van is a used-up man." Their plan worked. Harrison got slightly more votes than Van Buren in the popular election; in the electoral college, which officially chooses the president, Harrison's win was huge. He got 234 votes, and Van Buren got only 60 votes.

The Democrats had lost control of the White House, but they still controlled the U.S. Supreme Court. Seven of the nine justices on the court had been appointed years before by President Andrew Jackson. In their rulings these justices encouraged new businesses and attacked special privileges for the rich.

Harrison died a month after he took office. Vice President John Tyler replaced him. Tyler disagreed with other Whigs about how to handle the nation's problems. Because of this, the economic crisis dragged on. People no longer blamed Martin Van Buren for their problems.

## The Slavery Issue in the New Territories

By the election of 1844, slavery was becoming a major issue in northern states. The issue that most voters cared about, however, was how to make the nation bigger. An easy way to do this would be to make Texas a state, but slaves were being used in Texas.

Some people worried that making Texas a state would increase slavery in the nation. Other people didn't care about slavery. They simply wanted the United States to become bigger. They thought it was the nation's Manifest Destiny (a future event perceived as absolutely certain to happen) to possess all the land between the Atlantic and Pacific Oceans.

*Martin Van Buren (pictured) lost the 1844 Democratic presidential nomination to James K. Polk. Van Buren disagreed with most Democrats in not wanting to make statehood for Texas an issue.*

Martin Van Buren once again expected to get the nomination from the Democratic Party. He didn't want to make statehood for Texas an issue in the campaign because it would force him to take a stand on slavery. But most of the delegates at the Democratic Convention wanted Texas to become a state. They were unhappy that Van Buren wouldn't work to bring Texas into the Union.

When the delegates first voted for a presidential candidate, no one got a majority of the votes. They voted again, and still no one won. They voted nine times before they agreed on who their presidential candidate would be. Martin Van Buren lost. Instead, James K. Polk of Tennessee became the nominee.

The Democratic leaders didn't want the voters to think that they were favoring the South by picking a southerner as their candidate. So they were very careful when they wrote their **party platform.** A platform states what a political party wants to do if its candidates are elected.

In 1844 the Democratic platform had something for everyone. It talked about making Texas a state, which pleased people in the South. The platform also said that all of the Oregon country should belong to the United States. None of it should be given to England. People living in western states liked that idea. The Oregon country covered all the land west of the Great Divide, north of California, and into what is now Canada. When the election was over, Polk and the Democrats had won.

Because President Polk owned slaves, he didn't like people working to get rid of slavery. He warned that if slavery were outlawed, the nation would fall apart.

While James Polk was president, Texas became a state. President Polk also compromised with the British over how to split up the Oregon country. The British wanted everything north of the Columbia River, which runs between what are now the states of Washington and Oregon. The Americans wanted everything in the Oregon country. The two nations agreed to divide the Oregon country along the 49th parallel. That is still the boundary between the United States and Canada.

Polk also started a war with Mexico. The two countries disagreed over who controlled much of what is now the American Southwest. Many people did not like this war. They didn't think it was right to have soldiers dying over a land dispute.

When the United States won the war, there were more disagreements. Congress had to approve the treaty. Members of Congress couldn't do that, however, until they agreed on whether or not slaves would be allowed in the new territory.

Some of the leaders insisted slaves should be allowed. Others insisted just as strongly that no slaves should be allowed in new territories. A third group thought the people living in the territories should decide for themselves whether they wanted slaves. That way Congress wouldn't have to make decisions about slavery.

Before any decision was made, it was once again time to elect a president. The Democratic Party was divided into three groups. Some men from the South insisted on allowing slavery throughout the nation.

A group of men from New York called themselves the Barnburners. They had supported Martin Van Buren and wanted to get revenge for his loss of the election four years earlier. They chose their name because they wanted to clean house in the Democratic Party. Their name came from the saying that they were going to burn the barn to get rid of the rats.

A third group was called the Free-Soil Democrats. They wanted slavery kept out of any new territory the United States claimed. It would be "free soil," or land without slaves.

The divisions within the Democratic Party hurt it in the 1848 election. The Democrats lost the presidency to the Whig Party, which had **nominated** General Zachary Taylor, another war hero.

In 1850 Congress worked out a compromise over the issue of slavery. Some territories would be free, some territories would have slaves, and some territories would decide for themselves whether or not to allow slaves. People hoped this compromise would settle the issue forever.

Two years later the Democratic Party again won the election for president. They nominated Franklin Pierce from New Hampshire. Their platform endorsed the Compromise of 1850, which was very popular with voters.

## Intensification of the Slavery Issue

The fight over slavery continued. People began to physically attack each other over their views on slavery. Some people were killed. Senator Charles Sumner of Massachusetts made a speech against slavery. In it he made fun of Senator Pierce Butler of South Carolina, who had a speech problem because of a stroke.

Representative Preston Brooks was Senator Butler's nephew. He was so angry about the attack on his uncle that a few days later Representative Brooks beat Senator Sumner with a cane. The beating was so severe that Senator Sumner couldn't return to the Senate for years.

*Stephen Douglas (right) in one of his debates with Abraham Lincoln for the Illinois Senate. Douglas was the 1860 presidential candidate of the nonsouthern Democrats.*

Fights over slavery caused the Whig Party to fall apart. A new Republican Party, which was against slavery, formed. The Republicans could have won the election of 1856, but the Democratic Party carefully avoided taking any strong position on slavery. As a result, Democrat James Buchanan was elected president.

The issue of slavery refused to go away. People no longer debated the issue. They had decided where they stood. Violence spread, and more people were killed.

When the Democratic Party met in April for its 1860 convention, it was hopelessly divided over slavery. Northern Democrats supported Senator Stephen Douglas. He wanted new territories to decide for themselves whether to allow slaves. Southern Democrats insisted that slavery in new territories be protected by the government. Neither side would budge. They argued for days.

Finally, some Southern Democrats left the convention. Everyone else decided to try meeting again in June. They still couldn't agree. The party split. Southern Democrats held a separate convention. They nominated John C. Breckinridge for president. The other Democrats nominated Stephen Douglas.

Meanwhile, the Republican Party had nominated Abraham Lincoln for president. They insisted that slavery be kept within the states where it already existed. A new group called the Constitutional Union Party nominated John Bell.

Stephen Douglas became the first presidential candidate to personally campaign all over the country. He was able to use trains to travel from one area of the country to another. The popular vote was fairly close. But in the electoral college, Lincoln earned 180 votes, Douglas got only 12 votes, Breckinridge earned 72 votes, and Bell got 39 votes.

Southerners hated the idea of Abraham Lincoln becoming president. The stage was set for a brutal war. Decades would pass before the Democratic Party would be strong and united.

*Stephen Douglas was the first candidate to campaign all over the country. He traveled by train in the 1860 presidential election.*

*President Abraham Lincoln (left) and General George B. McClellan (right), who did not agree on military strategy during the Civil War, were also opponents in the 1864 presidential race.*

CHAPTER 3

# A Powerless Party

## The Civil War

SOME NORTHERN DEMOCRATS HATED the war with the South. They wanted Americans to work out their differences by talking. These people called themselves Peace Democrats.

Republicans had a different name for them; they called them Copperheads. They chose that name because copperhead snakes sneak up and strike without warning. They suspected the Peace Democrats were disloyal to the country. They accused them of spying and doing other things to help the South.

In reality only a few Northern Democrats worked for the South. Most Northern Democrats were not Copperheads at all. They called themselves War Democrats and agreed that war was necessary.

Many of the Democrats who lived in states such as Ohio, Indiana, and Illinois, however, were Copperheads. Their states were right next to the South. Some of their family members lived in Southern states.

Before the war, much of the money they earned came from selling things to Southerners.

Even though these Peace Democrats had so many ties to the South, most of them were loyal to the North. Nevertheless, the rumors that Democrats were spying for the South wouldn't go away.

In 1864 the war had been going on for three years. It was a big issue at the Democratic Convention that year. Copperheads were strong enough to control the party platform. They made sure that it said the war was a failure. It called for immediate peace talks with the South.

The party nominated George McClellan for president. He was a general who had led the Union army at the beginning of the war. McClellan disagreed with those who said that the war was a failure. He spoke against Democrats who wanted peace even if it led to dividing the country between North and South. He also criticized Republicans for saying that the war couldn't end until the South had freed all of its slaves.

At first it looked like President Lincoln might lose the election. Lots of soldiers had been killed. People were tired of war. But in late summer, the North won some important battles. That made the difference. The Democrats lost, and Lincoln returned to the White House.

Many Democrats were upset about the election. Union soldiers had been moved to areas where a lot of voters were Democrats. Many of the Peace Democrats in those areas had been afraid to vote because of the soldiers. Democrats didn't think it was fair that voting in the army took place only in units where most soldiers favored the Republicans.

By the end of the war, the names Copperhead and Democrat had come to mean the same thing throughout much of the North. For years the Democratic Party was linked with disloyalty during the war. The fact that most Democrats had supported both the Republican President Abraham Lincoln and the war didn't matter. People had heard so often about Copperheads working for the South that they believed it was true. Americans wouldn't elect a Democrat to the White House again until 1884.

## Reconstruction

The period immediately after the Civil War is called Reconstruction, because the South had to be rebuilt. Southern states had to rejoin the nation they had left at the beginning of the war. New leaders had to be elected, homes and buildings had to be rebuilt, and freed slaves needed homes and jobs. White farmers also had to figure out a new way to raise crops since they could no longer use slaves. Military governors ruled the Southern states while things got reorganized. Federal troops were stationed in the South to keep order and protect black people.

Americans were very angry after the war. Some people in the North wanted to make sure the Southern states were punished for starting a war. Some Southerners were angry about the way the Union army had destroyed their cities and farms. Many people were angry because their fathers, husbands, and sons had been killed in the war. With so many angry people, it was hard to bring the country together.

President Lincoln might have been able to get everyone to work together. He might have helped people forgive each other, but President Lincoln was shot and killed in 1865. Upon Lincoln's death, Vice President Andrew Johnson became the new president.

Andrew Johnson was originally from North Carolina. Although he was a Republican, he sympathized with the Southern farmers. He thought the Republicans were doing too much to protect the freed slaves. He thought they should be doing more to help the white Southern farmers and business owners.

*Republican President Andrew Johnson's sympathy for Southern farmers who had been impoverished during the war led him to work closely with the Democratic Party.*

Most Democrats wanted to help the white Southerners as well. So Andrew Johnson worked closely with the Democrats and ignored many people in his own party. He gave people he liked good jobs in the government. When he didn't like what people were doing, he took their jobs away.

The Republicans were upset that a Republican president wasn't doing what they wanted him to do. In 1868 the Republican majority in the House of Representatives voted unanimously to impeach the president. Johnson escaped conviction in the Senate by one vote. Not surprisingly, Republicans didn't nominate Andrew Johnson as their presidential candidate later that year. They chose the popular war hero Ulysses S. Grant. During the campaign, Republicans reminded voters about the rumors that the Democrats had helped the South during the war. The Democrats lost the election.

President Grant cared deeply about protecting the rights of blacks in the South, but he was not an effective president. People took advantage of him, including many of his advisors, who stole money from the government. Grant wouldn't listen to the advice of people who could have helped him solve some of the country's problems. Voters, however, didn't know about most of these things at the next election and so they reelected President Grant.

During the next four years things did not go well for Americans. Many people lost their jobs. People discovered that some Republicans had been stealing money from the government and they no longer trusted President Grant. The Democrats thought they would win the election in 1876.

The Democratic candidate, Samuel J. Tilden, got more votes than did Republican Rutherford B. Hayes. Both sides had cheated, though, and as a result, Tilden came up one vote short in the electoral college.

The Republicans and Democrats knew the country wouldn't survive a dispute over who had been elected president, so they made a deal. The Democrats would let Republican Rutherford B. Hayes become president. In exchange, the Republicans promised to get the federal troops out of the Southern states where they had been since the end of the Civil War. They would also fund railroad building and other improvements in the South.

Because of this agreement, white Southerners were once again in charge of their states. They knew that the Democratic Party had done this for them, and most of them voted for Democrats for about the next 80 years.

The agreement also meant that freed slaves in the South were no longer protected by soldiers. Groups such as the Ku Klux Klan began attacking black people more openly. When black men were given the right to vote in elections, they remembered that the Republican Party had fought the Civil War to free them. They also remembered that the Democratic Party had supported the white landowners. As a result, most black men voted for Republicans until the 1930s.

*Ku Klux Klansmen in Talluah, Louisiana, in 1962. When federal troops were withdrawn from the South after 1876, the Klan increased its attacks on black people. Its activities have continued to the present day.*

## The Bosses and Their Machines

During the 1870s cartoonists such as Thomas Nast began using the donkey as a symbol for the Democratic Party. Nast didn't like the Copperheads within the Democratic Party. He labeled a donkey in a cartoon as the Copperhead Press and showed it kicking a dead lion. The lion represented Secretary of War Edwin M. Stanton, who had just died. The public liked the donkey, so cartoonists continued using it. The Democrats still use that symbol today. The Republicans view the donkey as stubborn, silly, and ridiculous; the Democrats see it as humble, homely, courageous, and lovable.

The party also decided it needed a newspaper. In 1877 it started *The Washington Post* in Washington, D.C. (It sold the paper 12 years later.)

*A Thomas Nast cartoon showing Democratic congressmen as donkeys. The donkey became popular as the symbol for the Democratic Party during the 1870s.*

Political leaders continued giving jobs to their friends. In big cities such as New York and Chicago, powerful men, called bosses, ran the government. In some cities these bosses were Democrats. In others, they were Republicans.

The machines the bosses organized controlled who was elected to office. People who did what the bosses wanted were rewarded with jobs. Those who went against them lost power and money.

The bosses also gave themselves and their friends huge payments for work they hadn't done. In New York City a boss and his friends stole an estimated $30 million to $200 million from the city.

People were upset because the government wasn't working as well as it should be. The men who were being rewarded with government jobs often didn't know how to do the jobs they were hired for; because their jobs were rewards, they didn't get fired. No one had enough power to reform the system.

All this changed in 1881. Republican James Garfield had just taken office as president. Like the presidents before him, most of his time during the first few months in office was spent figuring out who should be rewarded with what job. One man didn't get the job he wanted. He was so angry that he shot President Garfield. On September 19, 1881, the president died from his wound.

When people heard why the president had been shot, they were shocked. They demanded that their leaders change the laws about government jobs. In 1883 the Pendleton Civil Service Act was passed. Introduced by Democratic Senator George Pendleton of Ohio, the law changed how people were hired for government jobs. It guaranteed that citizens could compete for some jobs simply based on their skills. Their politics, religion, race, or national origin couldn't be considered. At first the Civil Service Act affected only about 10 percent of government jobs, but it was a start to improving things.

The next year Democrats finally won a presidential election. Many Democrats wanted President Grover Cleveland to give as many jobs to people in their party as possible. Other Democrats wanted him to make every job appointment based on people's abilities. Cleveland did a little bit of each. This left both sides unhappy. President Cleveland lost the election in 1888, but he was reelected in 1892.

A short time after Grover Cleveland retook the presidency, the nation faced financial disaster. Wages were very low. People stopped buying things because they didn't have enough money. Shops closed because they didn't have customers. Lines of unemployed people waiting for a free bowl of soup became a common sight.

By 1896 things hadn't improved. Most Americans blamed the Democrats for their problems because the

Democrats were in power. The Democrats themselves couldn't agree on the best way to solve the problems.

At their convention in Chicago, they selected William Jennings Bryan as their candidate, but many Democrats didn't like Bryan's ideas, so they split from the party. Once again, the Democrats lost the election. As they headed toward a new century, they were still weak and divided.

*People suffering from the effects of the financial disaster of the 1890s often sought help from soup lines such as this one.*

*Steel workers in Pittsburgh, Pennsylvania, ca. 1905. Progressives from both parties wanted to make laws to protect workers from long hours and dangerous working conditions.*

CHAPTER **4**

# The Party Changes

## Social Issues

AT THE BEGINNING OF the 1900s, many people were trying to improve life in America. People often worked 12, 14, or 16 hours a day, 6 or 7 days a week. They didn't get paid if they had to stay home because they were sick. Sometimes the machines they worked with were dangerous. Even young children were forced to work in factories.

Some people, called Progressives, decided that the government needed to make laws to protect workers. Progressives were members of both the Republican and Democratic Parties.

One of the most famous Progressive presidents was Republican Teddy Roosevelt. When Roosevelt finished his two terms, Republican William Taft was elected. "Big Bill" Taft weighed about 300 pounds when he became president. He was very likeable, but he wasn't as good a politician as President Roosevelt. By the time Taft was finishing his first term, he knew he would not be reelected.

*When President William Taft again became the Republican presidential nominee in 1912, Theodore Roosevelt and his Progressive Party split from the Republican Party. The split allowed Democrat Woodrow Wilson to win the election.*

In 1912 the Republican Party split between people who supported and people who opposed the Progressive movement. This Republican split gave Democrats the first real chance since the Civil War to take power in both the White House and Congress. They nominated Woodrow Wilson for president.

Because the Progressives and their ideas had been forced out of the Republican Party, Wilson took those ideas for his own party. Democrats became known as the party of new ideas. From 1912 on, the Democratic Party began using government to make laws that improved working conditions, promoted racial equality, and addressed other social issues.

During the first part of the 1900s, Democrats also gained firm control of the political machines in urban areas. Big cities became strongholds of the Democratic Party. The bosses made sure people got out to vote and that they voted for Democrats.

Many people liked city bosses because they made sure that city government worked better than it had in the past.

In most cities, however, the leaders abused their power. In some cities the political machines kept various ethnic and minority groups from getting jobs. These tendencies gave city bosses and political machines a bad reputation.

Wilson won the election of 1912 easily. The energetic president began moving the country in new directions. Wilson addressed both houses of Congress in person—something that hadn't been done since Thomas Jefferson's day.

The new president got more laws passed during his first term than anyone expected. The income tax became law, and Wilson helped push through the Federal Reserve Act, which made banking safer and easier. The law created 12 districts across the nation. Each district has a federal reserve bank, and all are supervised by the Federal Reserve Board.

President Wilson didn't forget his concerns about working people. He helped get the Clayton Antitrust Act of 1914 passed. This act stated that strikes, boycotts, and picketing by workers were not against federal law. He also introduced laws to shorten the workday and to stop the exploitation of children in the workplace.

## World War I

Europe was at war, and many Americans were nervous that their country would join the war. The Democrats came up with the campaign slogan, "He kept us out of war!" They stressed that President Wilson had tried to keep America from taking sides in the conflict.

Even so, the election of 1916 was very close. When early returns showed the Republicans had swept the eastern states, even some Democratic newspapers admitted the Democrats had lost the election.

That was, however, before California's votes had been counted. When all the votes were in, President Wilson had 49.3 percent of the popular vote, and the Republican candidate, Charles Evans Hughes, had 46 percent of the popular vote.

*The British passenger liner* RMS Lusitania *was torpedoed and sunk by a German U-boat in 1915, killing 123 American passengers. Americans were outraged, and war with Germany was declared soon afterward.*

The electoral college vote was also close. Wilson got 277 electoral votes to Hughes's 254. It was the closest election in 50 years, with President Wilson the winner.

During his next term President Wilson could no longer keep the nation out of war. Several events helped to push the United States into the conflict. German U-boats sank unarmed U.S. merchant ships. Then the British intercepted a message from Germany to Mexico. The Germans promised Mexico that it would get New Mexico, Arizona, and Texas as a reward if it would join the war and fight against the United States. The British gave the message to America, and the American people were outraged. The result was that the United States went to war against Germany.

President Wilson had health problems during the last two years he was in office; the Democratic Party chose a new candidate, Ohio Governor James A. Cox. Cox, however, was defeated by Republican Warren G. Harding, who won more than 61 percent of the vote.

## Prohibition

During the next 12 years, Democratic Party leaders spent a lot of energy fighting each other. Southern Democrats supported Prohibition, the laws that made selling and drinking alcohol illegal. Northern Democrats from Irish,

German, and Italian backgrounds were against Prohibition. Responsible social drinking was part of their ethnic heritage. Neither side would budge.

That very issue was in part responsible for Democrat Al Smith's defeat in his run for president in 1928. He was the first Roman Catholic to get the nomination of a major party, as well as the first person who didn't have a farming background. Smith grew up in New York City. He worked in that city's Democratic political machine for years. From 1918 to 1928, he served as New York State's governor.

Smith campaigned for president all over the nation. In the big cities of the North and East, crowds of excited people greeted him. But most people in the South and the West did not like him. His Brooklyn accent and city ways didn't sit well with rural Americans. Voters in the South were also adamantly in favor of Prohibition, and Smith was opposed to it. In addition, times were good, and many voters saw no need to change things.

When the election was over, Al Smith carried all the big cities, but that wasn't enough to win. Republican Herbert Hoover won 58 percent of the popular vote. For the first time, Republicans had won the South.

The good times didn't last. In October 1929, the stock market crashed, and America entered the Great Depression.

*Wall Street during the stock market crash, October 1929. Decades of prosperity were coming to an end.*

*President Franklin D. Roosevelt, in one of his weekly "fireside chats," explains how a New Deal program will work. Roosevelt was a gifted speaker whose talks reassured many Americans.*

CHAPTER 5

# Democrats Take Charge

## The Great Depression

BY THE 1932 ELECTIONS, the United States faced serious problems. Between 25 and 30 percent of all workers were without jobs. Stocks were worth only about one-fifth of what they had been worth in 1929. Farmers had trouble finding places to sell their crops.

Americans were ready for a change. Republican President Hoover hadn't been able to fix their problems. Maybe someone else could.

Members of the Democratic Party realized they had a great opportunity. Whoever they named as their candidate for president would almost certainly get elected. Eight men wanted to be nominated.

The two men with the most support were "Cactus Jack" Garner and Franklin Delano Roosevelt. Garner, from Texas, was Speaker of the House of Representatives. Roosevelt, also called FDR, was governor of New York State.

One of Roosevelt's biggest supporters was Joseph P. Kennedy. Kennedy was a wealthy man who had taken his money out of the stock market before it crashed. He raised money for FDR and went to the Democratic Convention.

When it looked like there would be a tie between Roosevelt and Garner, Joseph Kennedy took action. Kennedy called up William Randolph Hearst, a wealthy publisher who controlled how the delegates from California voted. Kennedy convinced Hearst that if he didn't switch the support of California to Roosevelt, the convention would choose one of two men whom Hearst couldn't stand.

Hearst switched California's votes. Garner told the delegates who were supposed to vote for him that they could vote for someone else. These changes gave FDR enough votes to win the nomination. He rewarded Garner by selecting him to be his vice presidential running mate.

## FDR and the New Deal

Roosevelt campaigned over the radio. His speeches could be heard by everyone in the nation. FDR, a victim of polio, wore leg braces and couldn't walk without support. Some people thought he might be too weak to be president. To prove them wrong, Roosevelt traveled all over the country, visiting almost every state.

He was a gifted speaker with many ideas about how to fix the nation's problems. He promised a "New Deal" for the "forgotten man." On election day Roosevelt won 57.3 percent of the vote to President Hoover's 39.6 percent. His victory was even greater in the electoral college. There he got 472 votes to Hoover's 59.

When President Roosevelt took office, the nation faced unprecedented financial problems. Roosevelt made one of his most important speeches. "The only thing we have to fear is fear itself," he said. He persuaded many people that the government would be able to make their lives better.

Roosevelt was a smart politician. He knew it was important to keep the people's trust. So he started giving radio speeches each week. They were called "fireside chats." He wanted people to feel as if he were sitting in their living room by the fireplace and confiding in them. It worked. Many people became personally attached to the president.

Roosevelt also understood that he needed many different groups to support him. He got farmers, labor unions, ethnic minorities, liberals, intellectuals, and reformers to work together to solve the nation's problems. These groups of voters kept the Democratic Party in the White House for the next 20 years. Democrats also controlled one or both houses of Congress for most of the rest of the century.

To solve the nation's problems, Roosevelt invited many experts to Washington. He listened to their ideas and then created new government programs. These programs were named after the New Deal he had offered voters in his speeches.

Some of those programs are still part of American life. Social Security began as a New Deal program. Other

*Hoover Dam, one of the world's largest dams, was built between 1931 and 1936 by the U.S. Bureau of Reclamation with public works program laborers.*

programs put people to work constructing dams, bridges, roads, and public buildings.

Not everyone was happy with what FDR was doing. Some people lost all their money because of his policies. Nevertheless, the New Deal changed the way many people looked at government. The Democratic Party became known for developing programs to help people.

When it was time for the next presidential election, life had improved, but many people were still without jobs. Republicans claimed that the New Deal hadn't worked. Democrats said that without it, things would be even worse.

Most newspapers and businesspeople supported the Republican candidate, Alfred Landon. One poll predicted that Landon would win the 1936 election. But on election day President Roosevelt got 60.7 percent of the vote. He won 523 electoral votes out of a possible 531.

As he began his second term in office, FDR was ready to enlarge his New Deal programs. Critics wondered if these programs went against the Constitution. Eventually the U.S. Supreme Court ruled that parts of Roosevelt's New Deal went too far. Some of those programs ended. Others were changed.

As his second term came to an end, Roosevelt realized that wars in Europe and Asia would likely involve the United States before long. He also knew the American public wasn't ready to go to war, so he talked about doing things to help England that would be "short of war." This gave him the chance to build up the navy, which created more jobs.

FDR was very popular, but no president had ever run for a third term. They had followed the pattern set by George Washington, who retired after his second term.

At the 1940 Democratic Convention, he was nominated the first time the delegates voted, and he accepted in a radio speech. He said he had no right to refuse because of the dangerous situations in both Europe and Asia. His friends knew he was very happy to run for a third term.

## World War II

Once again, FDR won the election. He received 449 electoral votes to Republican Wendell Willkie's 82. Soon after his inauguration in 1941, Roosevelt pushed through a program that would let the United States send war supplies to England and its allies. Then, on December 7, the Japanese attacked Pearl Harbor, a U.S. naval base in the Hawaiian Islands. When the attack was over, 2,403 American military personnel and civilians had been killed.

The next day Congress declared war on Japan. Three days later, Germany and Italy declared war on the United States. President Roosevelt made a radio speech to the nation. "Never before has there been a greater challenge to life, liberty and civilization," he said.

The next four years were challenging. At times it seemed like the United States and its allies would lose. But in 1944, as another presidential election approached, it began to look as if the Allies might win the war.

*The battleship* USS Maryland *sinks during the Japanese attack on Pearl Harbor, December 7, 1941.*

Close friends and advisors of the president knew his health was failing, but they kept this news from the public. Roosevelt was once again nominated by the Democratic Convention. He and his advisors chose Senator Harry Truman of Missouri to be his running mate, suspecting that Roosevelt might not live to the end of his fourth term and that Truman would then become president.

Roosevelt and Truman were elected. Not long after, on April 12, 1945, President Roosevelt died. The nation was stunned. Truman was sworn into office and immediately began to bring World War II to an end. Less than a month later, on May 7, Germany signed an unconditional surrender to the Allied Forces in Europe.

War still raged in the Pacific, however. President Truman authorized the use of atomic bombs on two Japanese cities. Even then, Japanese military leaders did not want to surrender. Emperor Hirohito overruled his military advisors. On September 2, 1945, the Japanese signed surrender documents on the deck of the battleship *Missouri*.

## Postwar Problems

With the war over, problems at home began to surface. Women who worked during the war were told to let returning soldiers have their jobs. Because war equipment wasn't needed, people worked fewer hours and got paid less. The cost of food and other basic supplies increased about 25 percent.

In 1946 Republicans won a majority of the seats in both the House of Representatives and the Senate. When President Truman ran for office in 1948, no one expected him to win.

Truman came from a former slave state, but he wanted to guarantee civil rights for African Americans. He made sure that the Democratic platform included a strong statement about civil rights. This angered many Southern Democrats. They left the Democratic Party and formed their own party, the Dixiecrats.

The Republicans were eager to gain the presidency for the first time in 16 years. They nominated Governor Thomas Dewey of New York. Dewey worked hard to avoid making mistakes or stirring up controversy. This made him seem boring. Truman, on the other hand, gave energetic speeches and excited crowds everywhere.

First editions of morning newspapers the day after the election announced that Dewey had won. They were wrong. After Harry Truman won more than 50 percent of the popular vote to Dewey's 44 percent, he received 304 electoral votes to Dewey's 189.

After Harry Truman won a term as president on his own merits, he faced serious problems in both Europe and Asia. The Soviets, already in Czechoslovakia, blockaded West Berlin.

Then on June 25, 1950, North Korean armed forces swept into South Korea in an attempt to reunite the country under Communist leadership.

*President Harry S. Truman holds up the famous newspaper headline erroneously announcing that Thomas Dewey had won the 1948 election.*

*A soldier going into battle in Vietnam. The unpopularity of the war was a major factor in President Johnson's decision not to seek reelection in 1968.*

CHAPTER **6**

# Building for the Future

### The Korean War

KOREA HAD BEEN DIVIDED across the middle after World War II. The Soviet Union controlled the northern half; the United States occupied the southern half.

By 1948 both halves were independent nations. South Korea became the Republic of Korea, with a representative government. North Korea remained communist.

When North Korea attacked South Korea in 1950, it was supported by Communist China. General Douglas MacArthur commanded American troops in the Far East. He saw this as an opportunity to attack China.

America's allies were afraid that such action would lead to a third world war. President Truman repeatedly ordered General MacArthur to stay out of China. He also ordered the general not to make any public statements about the war without Truman's permission.

Instead, MacArthur publicly challenged the president's policy, something no military leader is allowed to do. On April 11, 1951, Truman relieved the general of his command.

The American public was outraged at this treatment of a popular war hero. Republican Senators Richard Nixon and Joseph McCarthy denounced Truman. Senator William E. Jenner threatened to have the president impeached. According to a Gallup poll, the public supported General MacArthur over President Truman by a 69 to 29 percent margin.

Truman did not seek the Democratic nomination in 1952. The war in Korea wasn't going well, and many people were terrified of the spread of Communism. They feared that the Soviet Union might attack at any moment.

These fears were fueled by Senate hearings conducted by Republican Senator Joseph McCarthy. He used a public relations firm to spread unsubstantiated charges against leading Democrats. Stories accused them of being "soft" on Communism and committing treason.

The Republicans nominated General Dwight Eisenhower for president. Eisenhower had no political experience, but he had led the Allied Forces to victory in Europe during World War II. Though not a good speaker, he was charming and trustworthy. People felt Eisenhower could win the war in Korea and protect them from Communism.

The Democrats nominated Illinois Governor Adlai Stevenson. He was known for his ideas, but most people found them too complex and impractical.

When the election was over, Eisenhower and his running mate, Richard Nixon, won 55.2 percent of the popular vote and 442 electoral votes. Stevenson received 44.5 percent of the popular vote and only 89 electoral votes.

## Civil Rights

Stevenson lost to Eisenhower again in 1956. Meanwhile, the Democratic Party still controlled Congress. One of the issues it addressed was civil rights.

*Rosa Parks is fingerprinted in Feb. 1956 after her arrest on charges of instigating a mass bus boycott in Montgomery, Alabama. The year-long boycott began after her initial arrest and release on Dec. 1, 1955, for refusing to sit at the back of the bus.*

Throughout the 1950s events drew national attention to the treatment of African Americans. In 1954 the U.S. Supreme Court ruled in *Brown v. Board of Education* that separate schools for black and white children were unconstitutional. The next year, Rosa Parks, a black woman, was arrested because she refused to sit in the back of a bus. Montgomery, Alabama, where she lived, required blacks to sit in the rear. Her arrest triggered peaceful protests.

In 1957 and 1960 Senator Lyndon B. Johnson, majority leader of the Democrats, oversaw the passage of the first civil rights bill in 85 years. The Democratic Party took up the fight for civil rights and gained many black supporters. At the same time, they lost votes among white southerners.

## John F. Kennedy's Policies

That black vote was critically important in the 1960 election. The Republicans nominated Vice President Richard Nixon as their candidate for president. The Democrats chose

John F. Kennedy, a young senator from Massachusetts. He was a son of Joseph P. Kennedy, who had helped Franklin Roosevelt get the party's nomination in 1932.

Kennedy was the first Roman Catholic to run for the presidency since Al Smith in 1928. His religious background and inexperience concerned some voters, but support began to grow after a series of debates with Nixon.

For the first time, presidential candidates debated on television. Nixon did not use makeup to compensate for the bright television lights. This made him look older and sickly. Kennedy came across as youthful, energetic, and full of new ideas.

In a very close race, Kennedy defeated Nixon. President Kennedy developed policies designed to reduce unemployment and provide medical care for the elderly. He also started the Peace Corps.

When the Soviet Union put a man in orbit around the earth, Kennedy declared that an American would reach the moon within a decade. He signed a treaty that banned testing nuclear weapons in the atmosphere. The treaty protected people from radiation.

Kennedy also made mistakes. Three months into office, he approved an invasion of Cuba that was designed to overthrow the government of Fidel Castro. The invasion force was defeated at the Bay of Pigs. This incident embarrassed Kennedy and increased tensions with the Soviet Union, an ally of Cuba.

In October 1962 the Soviets secretly began installing missile bases on Cuba. Such bases directly threatened the safety of Americans. Kennedy told the world what the Soviets were doing and forced the Soviets to remove the missiles. This successful act helped make up for the embarrassment of the Bay of Pigs.

President Kennedy introduced a Civil Rights Act in 1963 but was unable to get it through Congress. This failure was in part because he refused to make use of the political skills of his vice president, Lyndon Johnson. Johnson was a master at convincing members of Congress to vote for controversial bills.

On November 22, 1963, President Kennedy was assassinated in Dallas, Texas. Lyndon Johnson took the oath of office and became the next president.

## Lyndon Johnson's Domestic Programs

Johnson's skills in Congress helped him get the 1964 Civil Rights Act passed. It was tougher than the bill that Congress had rejected the previous year.

In November 1964, Johnson won a landslide victory over Republican Barry Goldwater. When Congress met two months later, Johnson introduced a program called the Great Society. Over the next two years, he persuaded Congress to pass most of it.

Johnson's plan included Medicare, which provided health care for the elderly. It also formed a cabinet-level department to oversee federal housing programs.

He declared a War on Poverty and provided funding to improve the economy in areas such as inner cities and Appalachia. Johnson also took steps to provide federal funding for elementary and secondary schools. Other programs cut water and air pollution.

## Vietnam War

The popularity of these programs was offset by the unpopularity of the Vietnam War. To many people, Vietnam was a war America couldn't win. This belief reinforced the perception that Democratic presidents couldn't win wars— a view that began when Truman was president.

The war became a major issue in the 1968 presidential election. After Senator Eugene McCarthy, a leading critic of the war, did well in the New Hampshire **primary,** Johnson announced he would not seek reelection.

Antiwar protesters at the Democratic Convention in Chicago shouted obscenities and threatened the police. The Chicago police responded by attacking the protesters and

*Police remove an antiwar protester during a demonstration that disrupted the Democratic National Convention in 1968.*

severely injuring many of them. Chaos erupted on the floor of the convention. In the end, the Democrats nominated Vice President Hubert Humphrey, but the party was bitterly divided.

Antiwar riots, race riots, and the assassinations that year of both Martin Luther King Jr., and Robert Kennedy fed the public perception that America stood on the brink of chaos. Humphrey lost the election to Republican Richard Nixon, but the Democrats held onto a large majority in both the House and the Senate.

## Republican Scandals

President Nixon and the Democratic Congress disagreed with each other on many issues. Nixon was successful in bringing an end to the Vietnam War and restoring relationships between the United States and the People's Republic of China. He also negotiated treaties with the Soviet Union.

After he was reelected in 1972, a story appeared about a robbery at the Democratic Party's headquarters at the Watergate apartment building in Washington, D.C. The Nixon administration tried to cover up its involvement in this robbery.

Congress held hearings. After months of investigation, it was clear that President Nixon faced impeachment and removal from office. Rather than undergo a Senate trial, Nixon resigned from office. Vice President Gerald Ford became the new president.

By the arrival of the 1976 election, voters were tired of Republican scandals. President Nixon had been forced from office. His original vice president, Spiro Agnew, had resigned after pleading no contest to charges of income tax evasion. Voters also wanted an end to high inflation and other economic problems.

## Democrats Regain Control

The Democratic Party knew it had an excellent chance to win back the White House. Many Democrats ran for the nomination. Jimmy Carter, the former governor of Georgia, won. He claimed that his inexperience in national government was a good thing. In a very close election, Carter defeated Gerald Ford with only 51 percent of the popular vote.

Once again, the Democrats controlled both the White House and Congress. But Jimmy Carter was not as skilled as Lyndon Johnson at working with Congress, and Democratic congressional leaders wanted to carry out their own agendas. Carter was unable to get Congress to pass his programs.

The president helped the peace process in the Middle East. He brought together President Anwar Sadat of Egypt and Prime Minister Menachem Begin of Israel. They signed the Camp David Accords, ending the state of war that had existed between their two countries since 1948.

*President Anwar Sadat of Egypt (right) and Prime Minister Menachem Begin of Israel (left) arrive at Camp David, Maryland, in 1978. The Camp David Accords were the first peace treaty between Israel and an Arab state.*

Carter also signed treaties that would give control of the Panama Canal to Panama at the end of 1999. He opened full diplomatic relations with China and signed treaties with the Soviet Union that limited the number of nuclear weapons.

On the domestic front, consumer prices continued to rise. Carter also faced a crisis in Iran, where, on November 4, 1979, Iranian students stormed the U.S. embassy and took American hostages. In 1980, Senator Edward Kennedy challenged Carter for the Democratic nomination for president. Carter managed to win, but the party was once again divided.

## The Reagan-Bush Years

Perhaps partly because of his inability to resolve the hostage situation, Carter lost the election to Republican candidate Ronald Reagan. The Iranians did not release their American hostages until the day Reagan took office.

One of the keys to Ronald Reagan's political success was his ability to label the Democrats as liberals who were out of touch with mainstream American values. This label stuck to the Democrats for the next 12 years.

## Bill Clinton, the "New Democrat"

In the 1992 election, Bill Clinton, former governor of Arkansas, ran for president by calling himself a "new Democrat." He convinced voters that he was a moderate and that Republicans were the extremists. He defeated Republican President George Bush, who was running for reelection.

Clinton supported international trade agreements, which are usually opposed by unions. He also worked to reduce federal spending on social programs. These actions moved the Democratic Party toward the political center and led to Clinton's reelection in 1996.

Personal scandals during the Clinton presidency reduced his influence on party leaders. At the same time, his moderate policies alienated long-time Democrats who believed that the government should do more to help and protect the American people.

The party founded by Jefferson and Madison continues to disagree over moderate and liberal solutions to the nation's problems. In the past, such disagreements have led to destructive splits within the party. To maintain their influence on American life into the 21st century, the party must find a way to maintain unity while engaging in vigorous and relevant debate.

# Glossary

**Campaign**—The process of rival candidates competing for public office.

**Candidate**—A person running for public office.

**Convention**—A meeting of party representatives who choose candidates, approve the party platform, and set party rules.

**Democracy**—A form of government in which every person has an equal say in what happens.

**Electoral college**—A group of people chosen by voters in each state to elect the president and vice president of the United States.

**Electoral vote**—The votes cast by the electoral college to select a president and vice president.

**Nominate**—To present a person as the best choice to be a party's candidate for political office.

**Party platform**—A series of statements that describes the goals and philosophy of a political party.

**Popular vote**—The votes cast by individual voters across the nation.

**Primary**—A statewide election in which party members vote for whom they want their party to nominate for political office.

**Republic**—A form of government in which leaders are elected rather than having inherited power or having taken it through force.

# Further Reading

Harvey, Miles. *Presidential Elections.* Chicago: Children's Press, 1996.

Henry, Christopher E. *Presidential Conventions.* New York: Franklin Watts, 1996.

Jones, Rebecca C. *The President Has Been Shot: True Stories of the Attacks on Ten U.S. Presidents.* New York: Puffin, 1998.

Mettger, Zak. *Reconstruction: America After the Civil War.* New York: Lodestar Books, 1994.

Sullivan, George. *Campaigns and Elections.* New York: Silver Burdett Press, 1991.

———. *Choosing the Candidates.* New York: Silver Burdett Press, 1991.

# Index

ABOUT THE AUTHORS: Bruce and Becky Durost Fish are freelance writers and editors who have worked on more than 100 books for children and young adults. They have degrees in history and literature and live in the high desert of Central Oregon.

SENIOR CONSULTING EDITOR Arthur M. Schlesinger, jr. is the leading American historian of our time. He won the Pulitzer Prize for his book *The Age of Jackson* (1945) and again for *A Thousand Days* (1965). This chronicle of the Kennedy Administration also won a National Book Award. Professor Schlesinger is the Albert Schweitzer Professor of the Humanities at the City University of New York, and has been involved in several other Chelsea House projects, including the REVOLUTIONARY WAR LEADERS and COLONIAL LEADERS series.

## Picture Credits

page
8 top: Archive Photos
8 bottom: Archive Photos
11: Archive Photos
14: Associated Press/
     University of Oregon
15: Archive Photos
16: Archive Photos
18: Archive Photos
20: Archive Photos
21: Archive Photos
24: Archive Photos
25: Archive Photos
26: Archive Photos
30: Archive Photos
32: AP/Wide World Photos
33: Archive Photos
35: American Stock/
     Archive Photos
36: Archive Photos
38: Hirz/Archive Photos
40: Archive Photos
41: Archive Photos
42: Archive Photos
45: Jeff Greenberg/
     Archive Photos
47: Scott Swanson/
     Archive Photos
49: Archive Photos
50: Archive Photos
53: AP/Wide World Photos
56: AP/Wide World Photos
58: Archive Photos